The very best 365 days

 @theverybest365days

ACKNOWLEDGMENTS

Chosen carefully, to generate your daily dose of motivation, each of these quotes can push you to be the best version of yourself.

Read, but not with the mind! Read with your soul, heart, and brain, and if you do that you are already one step closer to your goals!

I am grateful that this idea managed to become something tangible. I know that this book will not only be a simple reading but will become an important pillar in the growth and development of beautiful and successful characters. I am also grateful to:

Roberta, my best friend and also my wonderful fiancée, who always supported me and always managed to make me surpass myself and follow my dreams.

Radu and Florenta, my parents, who understood and supported me when I ran 2500km away to discover myself when nothing made sense at home.

Andrei, my friend, from whom I learned that you cultivate self-confidence with success, both big and small. And for the extraordinary work ethic I learned from him.

Leonard, my friend, from whom I learned that as long as you have a dream you have no time for anything else. I learned that if you really want something you have to give 110% regardless of the situation and what people say.

Cristian, my friend, from whom I learned that regardless of the situation and regardless of the person in front of you, you have to be fair to yourself and your values even if you can disturb certain people.

CONTENTS

People often say that motivation doesn't last. Neither does bathing; that's why we recommend it daily!

Zig Ziglar

1. **You don't have to be great to start, but you have to start to be great.**

   Zig Ziglar

2. **Success is a state of mind. If you want success, start thinking of yourself as a success.**

   Joyce Brothers

3. **Start wide, expand further, and never look back.**

   Arnold Schwarzenegger

4.   We should all start to live before we get too old.

Marilyn Monroe

5.   Start where you are. Use what you have. Do what you can.

Arthur Ashe

6. **Change your life today. Don't gamble on the future, act now without delay.**

   Simone de Beauvoir

7. **What you do today can improve all your tomorrows.**

   Ralph Marston

8. **The time is always right to do the right thing.**

   Martin Luther King Jr.

9. Life always begins with one step outside of your comfort zone.

Shannon L. Alder

10. Move out of your comfort zone. You can only grow if you are willing to feel awkward and uncomfortable when you try something new.

Brian Tracy

11. The secret to getting ahead is getting started.

Mark Twain

12. The beginning is always NOW.

Roy T. Bennett

13. I had as many doubts as anyone else. Standing on the starting line, we're all cowards.

Alberto Salazar

14. There are two fatal errors that keep great projects from coming to life:

   A) **Not finishing**

   B) **Not starting**

Buddha Gautama

15. Ideas don't come out fully formed, they only become clearer as you work on them. You just have to get started.

Mark Zuckerberg

16. Getting started is the most difficult thing to do; once you file it out, the rest of the journey is as soft as the straw. Be a good beginner.

Israelmore Ayivor

17. Every new beginning comes from some other beginning's end.

Lucius Annaeus Seneca

18. Everybody has to start from somewhere. You have your whole future ahead of you. Perfection doesn't happen right away.

Haruki Murakami

19. If everyone waited to become an expert before starting, no one would become an expert. To become an expert, you must have experience. To get experience, you must experiment! Stop waiting. Start stuff.

Richie Norton

20. Be willing to be a beginner every single morning.

Meister Eckhart

21. The beginning is always today!

Mary Shelley

22. The beginning is the most important part of the work.

Plato

23. No matter how short or long your journey to your accomplishment is, if you don't begin you can't get there. Beginning is difficult, but unavoidable!

Israelmore Ayivor

24. A vital part of the journey is the beginning. It is perhaps the most vital part.

Richelle E. Goodrich

25. Proven fact: You can never finish something you didn't start.

Sarah Knight

26. A new beginning comes from a new decision and vice versa.

Farley Maglaya

27. Do you want to know who you are? Don't ask. Act! Action will delineate and define you.

Thomas Jefferson

28. The path to success is to take massive, determined actions.

Tony Robbins

29. An idea not coupled with action will never get any bigger than the brain cell it occupied.

Arnold Glasow

30. God provides the wind, but man must raise the sails.

St. Augustine (Augustine of Hippo)

31. Be content to act and leave the talking to others.

Baltasar Gracian

32. Well done is better than well said.

Benjamin Franklin

33. Inaction breeds doubt and fear. Action breeds confidence and courage. If you want to conquer fear, do not sit home and think about it. Go out and get busy.

Dale Carnegie

34. Action is the antidote to despair.

Joan Baez

35. There is only one proof of ability: action!

Marie Ebner-Eschenbach

36. Action is a great restorer and builder of confidence. Inaction is not only the result, but the cause, of fear.

Norman Vincent Peale

37. Small deeds done are better than great deeds planned.

Peter Marshall

38. Take the first step in faith. You don't have to see the whole staircase, just take the first step.

Martin Luther King Jr.

39. Take action! An inch of movement will bring you closer to your goals than a mile of action.

Steve Maraboli

40. Start some when, somewhere or you won't reach anywhere.

Mystqx Skye

41. If you think you don't have enough time, that's ok, you have time enough now do!

Richie Norton

42. The longer you're not taking action the more money you're losing.

Carrie Wilkerson

43. Action is the foundational key to all success.

Pablo Picasso

44. One day or day one. You decide.

Unknown

45. Have enough courage to start and enough heart to finish.

Jessica N. S. Yourko

46. A ship is always safe at the shore, but that is not what it is built for.

Albert Einstein

47. The way to get started is to quit talking and begin doing.

Walt Disney

48. You miss 100 percent of the shots you don't take.

Wayne Gretzky

LET'S DO IT!

49. You can, you should, and if you're brave enough to start, you will.

Stephen King

50. A good plan violently executed now is better than a perfect plan executed next week.

George Patton

51. The key to success is to start before you are ready.

Marie Forleo

52. Be confident and courageous when you are about to make a start. Courage is the key!

Israelmore Ayivor

53. Believe in your potential. Your only limitations are those you set upon yourself.

Roy T. Bennett

54. We either make ourselves miserable, or we make ourselves strong. The amount of work is the same.

Carlos Castaneda

55. Only those who attempt the absurd can achieve the impossible.

Albert Einstein

56. In order to become strong tomorrow, stand up and fight today.

Yusuke Shirato

57. I charge you: once you have the dream, decide to begin and begin right away. Wait for nobody to blow whistles for you to start.

Israelmore Ayivor

58. Twenty years from now you will be more disappointed by the things you didn't do than by the ones you did do.

Mark Twain

59. Don't be too timid and squeamish about your actions. All life is an experiment.

Ralph Waldo Emerson

60. Great works are performed not by strength, but by perseverance.

Samuel Johnson

61. Either find a way or make one!

Hannibal B. Johnson

62. We like to think of our champions and idols as superheroes who were born different from us. We don't like to think of them as relatively ordinary people who made themselves extraordinary.

Carol S. Dweck

63. Always do what you are afraid of doing.

Ralph Waldo Emerson

64. All things are difficult before they are easy.

Thomas Fuller

65. If you find a path with no obstacles it probably doesn't lead anywhere.

Frank A. Clark

66. I am not afraid of storms for I am learning to sail my ship.

Louisa May Alcott

67. Confront your fear and turn the mental blocks into building blocks.

Dr. Roopleen

68. If you can't run, you crawl. If you can't crawl– you find someone to carry you.

Joss Whedon

69. The will of man is his happiness.

Johann Friedrich Von Schiller

70. Men can do all things if they will.

Leon Batista Alberti

71. Where the willingness is great, the difficulties cannot be great.

Niccolò Machiavelli

72. You are the only person on earth who can use your ability.

Zig Ziglar

73. Willpower gets you started. Habits get you results.

Priit Kallas

74. Strength does not come from physical capacity. It comes from an indomitable will.

Mahatma Gandhi

75. I am, indeed, a king, because I know how to rule myself.

Pietro Aretino

76. Willpower is essential to the accomplishment of anything worthwhile.

Brian Tracy

77. What you have to do and the way you have to do it is incredibly simple. Whether you are willing to do it, that's another matter.

Peter F. Drucker

78. The more things you do, the more you can do.

Lucille Ball

79. I don't wait for moods. You accomplish nothing if you do that. Your mind must know it has got to get down to work.

Pearl S. Buck

80. Nothing is easy to the unwilling.

Thomas Fuller

81. You are only as lazy or lacking in willpower as you think you are.

Ken Christian

82. To assert your willpower is simply to make up your mind that you want something, and then refuse to be put off.

Phillip Cooper

83. In the absence of willpower, the most complete collection of virtues and talents is wholly worthless.

Aleister Crowley

84. Willpower is the key to success. Successful people strive no matter what they feel by applying their will to overcome apathy, doubt or fear.

Dan Millman

85. What is now proved was once only imagined.

William Blake

86. Nothing can withstand the power of the human will if it is willing to stake its very existence to the extent of its purpose.

Benjamin Disraeli

87. The best way to think of willpower is not as some shapeless behavioral trait but as a sort of psychic muscle, one that can atrophy or grow stronger depending on how it's used.

Jeffrey Kluger

88. Most of life's actions are within our reach, but decisions take willpower.

Robert McKee

89. True success comes from failing repeatedly and as quickly as possible, before your cash or your willpower runs out.

Jay Samit

90. We all have the power of thought - so what are you lacking? If you have willpower, then you can change anything.

Dalai Lama

91. Where there's a will, there's a way. Perhaps tomorrow, if not today.

Michele Jennae

92. People with a strong will power will always have the bigger picture in mind. They will be able to forget small pleasures in order to help attain bigger goals.

Brian Adams

93. If we have the willpower and desire to create something, we have to wait patiently to see the results as they grow, day by day.

Ratna Joshi

94. You may encounter many disappointments. Be strong. Tell yourself, "I am good enough, I will try again."

Lailah Gifty Akita

95. With motivation you get willpower, and with willpower you get the strength to work hard for what you want.

Fred Juliusson

96. Changing a habit requires determination, perseverance and a strong will power.

Catherine Pulsifer

97. Changing your negative thoughts into positive ones is difficult but not impossible to do. It only requires two things: willpower and determination.

Alexi Weaver

98. One is never born great. It is the will power and the action, that make one great.

M.K. Soni

99. Once you reach the brink of your will power, you have two options - either give up, or keep going. That decision decides whether you'll reach your goal.

Abhijit Naskar

100. If you are willing to be a self-learner, you will develop yourself.

Lailah Gifty Akita

101. A heart full of love and compassion is the main source of inner strength, willpower, happiness, and mental tranquility.

Dalai Lama

102. Don't say you don't have enough time. You have exactly the same number of hours per day that were given to Helen Keller, Pasteur, Michelangelo, Mother Teresa, Leonardo Da Vinci, Thomas Jefferson, and Albert Einstein.

H. Jackson Brown Jr.

103. The best time to plant a tree was 20 years ago. The second-best time is now.

Chinese Proverb

104. There's no shortage of remarkable ideas, what's missing is the will to execute them.

Seth Godin

105. Never lose hope. Storms make people stronger and never last forever.

Roy T. Bennett

106. It does not matter how slowly you go as long as you do not stop.

Andy Warhol

107. Don't give up when dark times come. The more storms you face in life, the stronger you'll be. Hold on. Your greater is coming.

Germany Kent

108. I may not be where I want to be, but if I stop now, I'll never get where I'm going!

Laura Lynch

109. Never give up, for that is the place and time that the tide will turn.

Harriet Beecher

110. No matter how hard it is, try to be stronger than yesterday.

Shaa Zainol

111. Despite how dark it might be, what is tonight but the precursor to tomorrow?

Craig D. Lounsbrough

112. Challenges are gifts that force us to search for a new center of gravity. Don't fight them. Just find a new way to stand.

Oprah Winfrey

113. I don't count my sit-ups; I only start counting when it starts hurting because they're the only ones that count.

Muhammad Ali

114. If you're going through hell, keep going.

Winston Churchill

115. Most of the important things in the world have been accomplished by people who have kept on trying when there seemed no hope at all.

Dale Carnegie

116. Our greatest weakness lies in giving up. The most certain way to succeed is always to try just one more time.

Thomas Edison

117. The best way to treat obstacles is to use them as stepping-stones. Laugh at them, tread on them, and let them lead you something better.

Enid Blyton

118. Challenges are what make life interesting, overcoming them is what makes life meaningful.

Joshua J. Marine

119. Just because you haven't found your talent yet doesn't mean you don't have one.

Kermit the Frog

120. It's hard to beat a person that never gives up.

Babe Ruth

121. If you quit once it becomes a habit, don't quit!

Michael Jordan

122. Do not be embarrassed by your failures, learn from them and start again.

Richard Branson

123. Ever tried. Ever failed. No matter. Try Again. Fail again. Fail better.

Samuel Beckett

124. I've missed more than 9,000 shots in my career. I've lost almost 300 games. 26 times I've been trusted to take the game winning shot and missed. I've failed over and over and over again in my life and that is why I succeed.

Michael Jordan

125. The hard days are what make you stronger.

Aly Raisman

126. Never stop doing your best just because someone doesn't give you credit.

Kamari aka Lyrikal

127. If something is important enough, even if the odds are stacked against you, you should still do it.

Elon Musk

128. Tough times never last but tough people do.

Robert H. Schuller

129. Energy and persistence conquer all things.

Benjamin Franklin

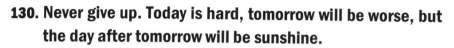

130. Never give up. Today is hard, tomorrow will be worse, but the day after tomorrow will be sunshine.

Jack Ma

131. I have not failed. I've just found 10,000 ways that won't work.

Thomas Edison

132. Challenges are what make life interesting and overcoming them is what makes life meaningful.

Joshua J. Marine

133. Perseverance is failing 19 times and succeeding the 20th.

Julie Andrews

134. Problems are not stop signs; they are guidelines.

Robert H. Schuller

135. Our greatest glory is not in never falling but in rising every time we fall.

Confucius

136. Go as far as you can see; when you get there, you'll be able to see further.

Thomas Carlyle

137. You learn more from failure than from success. Don't let it stop you. Failure builds character.

Unknown

138. A river cuts through rock, not because of its power but because of its persistence.

Jim Watkins

139. If you can't fly, then run. If you can't run, then walk. If you can't walk, then crawl, but whatever you do, you have to keep moving forward.

Martin Luther King, Jr.

140. Obstacles don't have to stop you. If you run into a wall, don't turn around and give up.

Michael Jordan

141. You are never too old to set another goal or to dream a new dream.

C. S. Lewis

142. Many of life's failures are people who did not realize how close they were to success when they gave up.

Thomas Edison

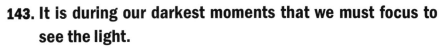

143. It is during our darkest moments that we must focus to see the light.

Aristotle Onassis

144. You will never reach your destination if you stop and throw stones at every dog that barks.

Winston Churchill

145. Go the extra mile. It's never crowded there.

Dr. Wayne W. Dyer

146. Sometimes when you're in a dark place you think you've been buried but you've actually been planted.

Christine Caine

147. Turn your wounds into wisdom.

Oprah Winfrey

148. When written in Chinese the word "crisis" is composed of two characters – one represents danger and the other represents opportunity.

John F. Kennedy

149. The most common way people give up their power is by thinking they don't have any.

Alice Walker

150. You may have to fight a battle more than once to win it.

Margaret Thatcher

151. A man is not finished when he is defeated. He is finished when he quits.

Richard Nixon

152. Falling down is how we grow. Staying down is how we die.

Brian Vaszily

153. Defeat is a state of mind; no one is ever defeated until defeat is accepted as a reality.

Bruce Lee

154. Character consists of what you do on the third and fourth tries.

James A. Michener

155. It always seems impossible until it's done.

Nelson Mandela

156. You can't let your failures define you. You have to let your failure teach you.

Barack Obama

157. Develop a passion for learning. If you do, you will never cease to grow.

Anthony J. D'Angelo

158. If you are not willing to learn, no one can help you. If you are determined to learn, no one can stop you.

Zig Ziglar

159. The more you learn, the more you earn.

Warren Buffett

160. An expert is a person who has made all the mistakes that can be made in a very narrow field.

Niels Bohr

161. Love challenges, be intrigued by mistake, enjoy effort and keep on learning.

Carol S. Dweck

162. Live as if you were to die tomorrow. Learn as if you were to live forever.

Mahatma Gandhi

163. Wisdom is not a product of schooling but of the lifelong attempt to acquire it.

Albert Einstein

164. One learns from books and example only that certain things can be done. Actual learning requires that you do those things.

Frank Herbert

165. One hour per day of study in your chosen field is all it takes. One hour per day of study will put you at the top of your field within three years. Within five years you'll be a national authority. In seven years, you can be one of the best people in the world at what you do.

Earl Nightingale

166. You don't understand anything until you learn it more than one way.

Marvin Minsky

167. He who laughs most, learns best.

John Cleese

168. Anyone who stops learning is old, whether at twenty or eighty. Anyone who keeps learning stays young. The greatest thing in life is to keep your mind young.

Henry Ford

169. Study hard what interests you the most in the most undisciplined, irreverent and original manner possible.

Richard Feynman

170. The beautiful thing about learning is nobody can take it away from you.

B.B. King

171. I am still learning.

Michelangelo

172. I never learned from a man who agreed with me.

Robert A. Heinlein

173. You don't learn to walk by following rules. You learn by doing, and by falling over.

Richard Branson

174. The whole purpose of education is to turn mirrors into windows.

Sydney J. Harris

175. Curiosity is the wick in the candle of learning.

William Arthur Ward

176. Leadership and learning are indispensable to each other.

John F. Kennedy

177. Any fool can know. The point is to understand.

Albert Einstein

178. You aren't learning anything when you're talking.

Lyndon B. Johnson

179. The quieter you become, the more you can hear.

Gautama Buddha

180. By three methods we may learn wisdom: First, by reflection, which is noblest; Second, by imitation, which is easiest; and third by experience, which is the bitterest.

Confucius

181. Knowing is not enough; We must apply. Willing is not enough; We must do.

Bruce Lee

182. It is not that I'm so smart. But I stay with the questions much longer.

Albert Einstein

183. The more that you read, the more things you will know. The more that you learn, the more places you'll go.

Dr. Seuss

184. Those who don't know history are doomed to repeat it.

Edmund Burke

185. Never let hard lessons harden your heart; the hard lessons of life are meant to make you better, not bitter.

Roy T. Bennett

186. Learning never exhausts the mind.

Leonardo da Vinci

187. Learning is not child's play; we cannot learn without pain.

Aristotle

188. Formal education will make you a living; self-education will make you a fortune.

Jim Rohn

189. Learn everything you can, anytime you can, from anyone you can, there will always come a time when you will be grateful you did.

Sarah Caldwell

190. What I learned on my own I still remember.

Nassim Nicholas Taleb

191. Practice is the hardest part of learning, and training is the essence of transformation.

Ann Voskamp

192. The mind is just like a muscle - the more you exercise it, the stronger it gets and the more it can expand.

Idowu Koyenikan

193. You will either step forward into growth, or you will step backward into safety.

Abraham Maslow

194. It is impossible for a man to learn what he thinks he already knows.

Epictetus

195. If a man empties his purse into his head, no man can take it away from him. An investment in knowledge always pays the best interest.

Benjamin Franklin

196. We learn more by looking for the answer to a question and not finding it than we do from learning the answer itself.

Lloyd Alexander

197. Things may come to those who wait, but only the things left by those who hustle.

Abraham Lincoln

198. If you hear a voice within you say, 'you cannot paint,' then by all means paint and that voice will be silenced.

Vincent Van Gogh

199. The function of leadership is to produce more leaders, not more followers.

Ralph Nader

200. Reading is to the mind, as exercise is to the body.

Brian Tracy

201. Smart people learn from everything and everyone, average people from their experiences, stupid people already have all the answers.

Socrates

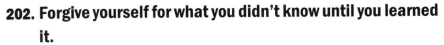

202. Forgive yourself for what you didn't know until you learned it.

Zig Ziglar

203. Reading is to the mind, as exercise is to the body.

Brian Tracy

204. Thinking should become your capital asset, no matter whatever ups and downs you come across in your life.

A. P. J. Abdul Kalam

205. A wise man can learn more from a foolish question than a fool can learn from a wise answer.

Bruce Lee

206. Learn as though you would never be able to master it; hold it as though you would be in fear of losing it.

Confucius

207. Those people who develop the ability to continuously acquire new and better forms of knowledge that they can apply to their work and to their lives will be the movers and shakers in our society for the indefinite future.

Brain Tracy

208. Education is not the filling of a pail, but the lighting of a fire.

W.B. Yeats

209. The more you feed your mind with positive thoughts, the more you can attract great things into your life.

Roy T. Bennett

210. Our life is what or thoughts make it.

Marcus Aurelius

211. Once your mindset changes, everything on the outside will change along with it.

Steve Maraboli

212. Discipline is giving yourself a command and following it up with action.

Bob Proctor

213. If the seed doesn't get planted, it can't become a toxic thorn bush. We must guard our minds and our hearts, starting with our eyes.

Craig Groeschel

214. Motivation may be what starts you off, but it's habit that keeps you going back for more.

Miya Yamanouchi

215. Do. Then talk. In that order!

Sotero M. Lopez II

216. It is not true the people stop pursuing dreams because they grow old. They grow old because they stop pursuing dreams.

Gabriel Garcia Marquez

217. You can't have a million-dollar dream with a minimum-wage work ethic.

Stephen C. Hogan

218. Don't be afraid to give up the good to go for the great.

John D. Rockefeller

219. Show me your crowd, I'll show you your future.

Ray Lewis

220. There's no such things as failure. Only results.

Tony Robbins

221. I like criticism. It makes you strong.

LeBron James

222. Success is no accident. It is hard work, perseverance, learning, studying, sacrifice, and most of all, love of what you are doing or learning to do.

Pele

223. Look for the good in every situation. Seek the valuable lesson in every setback. Look for the solution to every problem. Think and talk continually about your goals.

Brian Tracy

224. Every endeavor pursued with passion produces a successful outcome regardless of the result. For it is not about winning or losing. Rather the effort put forth into producing the outcome. The best way to predict the future is to create it.

Nick Bollettieri

225. Attitude is a little thing that makes a big difference.

Winston Churchill

226. A truly strong person does not need the approval of others any more than a lion needs the approval of sheep.

Vernon Howard

227. Believe you can...and you are halfway there!

Theodore Roosevelt

228. Important achievements require a clear focus, all-out effort, and a bottomless trunk full of strategies, plus allies in learning.

Carol S. Dweck

229. What you think, you become. What you feel, you attract. What you imagine, you create.

Gautama Buddha

230. Ideas without action aren't ideas. They're regrets.

Steve Jobs

231. Happiness depends on your mindset and attitude.

Roy T. Bennett

232. Once your mindset changes, everything on the outside will change along with it.

Steve Maraboli

233. My dad encouraged us to fail. Growing up, he would ask us what we failed at that week. If we didn't have something, he would be disappointed. It changed my mindset at an early age that failure is not the outcome, failure is not trying. Don't be afraid to fail.

Sara Blakely

234. Open the window of your mind. Allow the fresh air, new lights and new truths to enter.

Amit Ray

235. No matter what, people grow. If you chose not to grow, you're staying in a small box with a small mindset. People who win go outside of that box. It's very simple when you look at it.

Kevin Hart

236. I think anything is possible if you have the mindset and the will and desire to do it and put the time in.

Roger Clemens

237. Leadership is a mindset that shifts from being a victim to creating results. Any one of us can demonstrate leadership in our work and within our lives.

Robin S. Sharma

238. Eliminate the mindset of CAN'T! Because you can do anything!

Tony Horton

239. Anyone can train to be a gladiator. What marks you out is having the mindset of a champion.

Manu Bennett

240. I truly believe in positive synergy, that your positive mindset gives you a more hopeful outlook, and belief that you can do something great means you will do something great.

Russell Wilson

241. Nothing is impossible. The word itself says "I'm possible".

Audrey Hepburn

242. It takes a different mindset to be successful in anything; that's why there's not a lot of super-duper successful people, because it's guys I know who may be ten times more talented than me, but they don't work as hard.

Rico Love

243. Success is the ability to go from one failure to another with no loss of enthusiasm.

Winston Churchill

244. Anyone who has never made a mistake has never tried anything new.

Albert Einstein

245. Never limit yourself because of others' limited imagination; never limit others because of your own limited imagination.

Mae Jemison

246. Your attitude, not your aptitude, will determine your altitude.

Zig Ziglar

247. If you are not willing to risk the usual, you will have to settle for the ordinary.

Jim Rohn

248. To live a creative life, we must lose our fear of being wrong.

Joseph Clinton Pearce

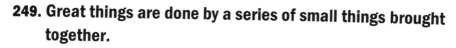

249. Great things are done by a series of small things brought together.

Vincent Van Gogh

250. Setting goals is the first step in turning the invisible into the visible.

Tony Robbins

251. Whether you think you can, or you think you can't — You're right.

Henry Ford

252. You have to believe in yourself when no one else does.

Venus Williams

253. The successful warrior is the average man, with laser like focus.

Bruce Lee

254. The No. 1 reason people fail in life is because they listen to their friends, family, and neighbors.

Napoleon Hill

255. When everything seems to be going against you, remember that the airplane takes off against the wind, not with it.

Henry Ford

256. Student says: "I'm very discouraged. What should I do?" Master says: "Encourage others.

Zen Proverb

257. If you realized how powerful your thoughts are, you would never think a negative thought.

Peace Pilgrim

258. Don't limit yourself. Many people limit themselves to what they think they can do. You can go as far as your mind lets you. What you believe, remember, you can achieve.

Mary Kay Ash

259. Life is 10% what happens to me and 90% of how I react to it.

Charles Swindoll

260. Leaders must be close enough to relate to others, but far enough ahead to motivate them.

John C. Maxwell

261. If you have a dream, don't just sit there. Gather courage to believe that you can succeed and leave no stone unturned to make it reality.

Dr. Roopleen

262. Create a vision for the life you really want and then work relentlessly towards making it a reality.

Roy T. Bennett

263. Outstanding people have one thing in common: an absolute sense of mission.

Zig Ziglar

264. You are what you do, not what you say you do.

Carl Jung

265. Greatness only comes before hustle in the dictionary.

Ross Simmonds

266. Some people want it to happen, some people wish it would happen, others make it happen.

Michael Jordan

267. The hustle brings the dollar. The experience brings the knowledge. The persistence brings the success.

Ross Simmonds

268. Don't stay in bed unless you can make money in bed.

George Burns

269. It's not about money or connections. It's the willingness to outwork and outlearn everyone when it comes to your business.

Mark Cuban

270. The dream is free. The hustle is sold separately.

Unknown

271. Talent is cheaper than table salt. What separates the talented individual from the successful one is a lot of hard work.

Stephen King

272. Work hard now. Don't wait. If you work hard enough, you'll be given what you deserve.

Shaquille O'Neal

273. Dreams don't work unless you do.

John C. Maxwell

274. If people knew how hard I had to work to gain my mastery, it would not seem so wonderful at all.

Michelangelo

275. There is no elevator to success. You have to take the stairs.

Zig Ziglar

276. It's kind of fun to do the impossible.

Walt Disney

277. Every successful person in the world is a hustler one way or another. We all hustle to get where we need to be. Only a fool would sit around and wait on another man to feed him.

K'wan Foye

278. The only difference between ordinary and extraordinary is that little extra.

Jimmy Johnson

279. I wake up every morning and think to myself, 'how far can I push this company in the next 24 hours.

Leah Busque

280. There is no substitute for hard work.

Thomas Edison

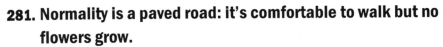

281. Normality is a paved road: it's comfortable to walk but no flowers grow.

Vincent van Gogh

282. When there is no struggle, there is no strength.

Oprah Winfrey

283. Opportunities don't happen, you create them.

Chris Grosser

284. Things do not happen. Things are made to happen.

John F. Kennedy

285. I find that the harder I work, the more luck I seem to have.

Thomas Jefferson

286. Working hard for something we don't care about is called stressed; working hard for something we love is called passion.

Simon Sinek

287. I didn't get there by wishing for it or hoping for it, but by working for it.

Estée Lauder

288. Always make a total effort, even when the odds are against you.

Arnold Palmer

289. Success usually comes to those who are too busy to be looking for it.

Henry David Thoreau

290. For 37 years I've practiced 14 hours a day, and now they call me a genius.

Pablo de Sarasate

291. Work like there is someone working twenty-four hours a day to take it away from you.

Mark Cuban

292. Amateurs sit around and wait for inspiration. The rest of us just get up and go to work.

Stephen King

293. If you work on something a little bit every day, you end up with something that is massive.

Kenneth Goldsmith

294. Work hard for what you want because it won't come to you without a fight. You have to be strong and courageous and know that you can do anything you put your mind to. If somebody puts you down or criticizes you, just keep on believing in yourself and turn it into something positive.

Leah LaBelle

295. A surplus of effort could overcome a deficit of confidence.

Sonia Sotomayor

296. You can control two things: your work ethic and your attitude about anything.

Ali Krieger

297. What you lack in talent can be made up with desire, hustle and giving 110% all the time.

Don Zimmer

298. Live daringly, boldly, fearlessly. Taste the relish to be found in competition – in having put forth the best within you.

Henry J Kaiser

299. Contrary to popular opinion, the hustle is not a dance step – it's an old business procedure.

Fran Lebowitz

300. When I started flirting with the hustle, failure became my ex. Now engaged to the game and married to success.

Unknown

301. When I was young, I observed that nine out of 10 things I did were failures. So, I did 10 times more work.

George Bernard Shaw

302. Those at the top of the mountain didn't fall there.

Marcus Washling

303. He who is outside his door has the hardest part of his journey behind him.

Dutch Proverb

304. All life demands struggle. Those who have everything given to them become lazy, selfish and insensitive to the real values of life. The very striving and hard work that we so constantly try to avoid is the major building block in the person we are today.

Pope Paul VI

305. I love people, and the hustle.

Gary Vaynerchuk

306. Hard work never killed a man.

Scottish proverb

307. The fruit of your own hard work is the sweetest.

Deepika Padukone

308. There's a difference between fake hustle for show and being someone who tries hard to win.

Manny Machado

309. Everyone is where they are at because they worked hard for it. Don't ever hate on someone's hustle. Just figure out how you can get there.

Jo Koy

310. I love the work, love the grind. I love what I have to go through to get what I want.

Deshaun Watson

311. Grind until you get it no matter what the haters say and never look back, keep striving cause it's your life.

Jonathan Anthony Burkett

312. Today, I will do what others won't, so tomorrow I can accomplish what others can't.

Jerry Rice

313. You're going to make it; you're going to be at peace; you're going to create, and love, and laugh, and live; you're going to do great things.

Germany Kent

314. People may doubt what you say, but they will believe what you do.

Lewis Cass

315. Success isn't always about greatness. It's about consistency. Consistent hard work gains success. Greatness will come.

Dwayne Johnson

316. It's not too late to start! Start right now anyway. Set goals and take action. Have courage to fall, fail and suffer. Don't quit. Persist with courage. Success will achieve anyway and be yours 100% guaranteed.

Lord Robin Russell

317. Let your performance do the thinking.

Charlotte Bronte

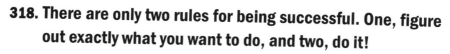

318. There are only two rules for being successful. One, figure out exactly what you want to do, and two, do it!

Mario Cuomo

319. We are what we repeatedly do. Excellence, then, is not an act, but a habit.

Aristotle

320. It is hard to fail but it is worse never to have tried to succeed.

Theodore Roosevelt

321. If you don't give anything don't expect anything. Success is not coming to you; you must come to it.

Marva Collins

322. Failure is so important. We speak about success all the time. But it is the ability to resist or use failure that often leads to greater success.

J. K. Rowling

323. Success is not an accident; success is a choice.

Stephen Curry

324. Your time is limited, so don't waste it living someone else's life.

Steve Jobs

325. If you cannot do great things, do small things in a great way.

Napoleon Hill

326. Success means doing the best we can with what we have. Success is the doing, not the getting; in the trying, not the triumph. Success is a personal standard, reaching for the highest that is in us, becoming all that we can be.

Zig Ziglar

327. One day the people that don't even believe in you will tell everyone how they met you.

Johnny Depp

328. If I'm gonna tell a real story, I'm gonna start with my name.

Kendrick Lamar

329. Don't wait for the perfect conditions for success to happen; just go ahead and do something.

Dan Miller

330. Successful people do what unsuccessful people are not willing to do. Don't wish it were easier; wish you were better.

Jim Rohn

331. I cannot give you a formula for success, but I can give you the formula for failure, which is: Try to please everybody.

Herbert Bayard Swope

332. Take up one idea. Make that one idea your life-think of it, dream of it, live on that idea. Let the brain, muscles, nerves, every part of your body, be full of that idea, and just leave every other idea alone. This is the way to success.

Swami Vivekananda

333. Success is walking from failure to failure with no loss of enthusiasm.

Winston Churchill

334. Success is not the key to happiness. Happiness is the key to success. If you love what you are doing, you will be successful.

Albert Schweitzer

335. Success is not final; failure is not fatal: it is the courage to continue that counts.

Winston Churchill

336. No one is to blame for future situation but yourself. If you want to be successful, then become successful.

Jaymin Shah

337. Would you like me to give you a formula for success? It's quite simple, really: Double your rate of failure. You are thinking of failure as the enemy of success. But it isn't at all. You can be discouraged by failure or you can learn from it, so go ahead and make mistakes. Make all you can. Because remember that's where you will find success.

Thomas J. Watson

338. We need to accept that we won't always make the right decisions, that we'll screw up royally sometimes – understanding that failure is not the opposite of success, it's part of success.

Arianna Huffington

339. There are two rules for success. 1: Never reveal everything you know.

Roger H. Lincoln

340. Try not to become a man of success. Rather become a man of value.

Albert Einstein

341. I owe my success to having listened respectfully to the very best advice, and then going away and doing the exact opposite.

G. K. Chesterton

342. People who succeed have momentum. The more they succeed, the more they want to succeed, and the more they find a way to succeed. Similarly, when someone is failing, the tendency is to get on a downward spiral that can even become a self-fulfilling prophecy.

Tony Robbins

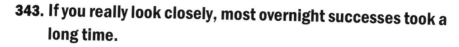

343. If you really look closely, most overnight successes took a long time.

Steve Jobs

344. There are no secrets to success. It is the result of preparation, hard work, and learning from failure.

Colin Powell

345. Success seems to be connected with action. Successful people keep moving. They make mistakes, but they don't quit.

Conrad Hilton

346. A successful man is one who can lay a firm foundation
with the bricks that other throw at him.

David Brinkley

347. The secret of success is to do the common thing
uncommonly well.

John D. Rockefeller Jr.

348. For every reason it's not possible, there are hundreds of people who have faced the same circumstances and succeeded.

Jack Canfield

349. I think goals should never be easy, they should force you to work, even if they are uncomfortable at the time.

Michael Phelps

350. Success in general is a well-balanced blend of luck, DNA, confidence, and hustle.

Gary Vaynerchuk

351. Ambition is the path to success. Persistence is the vehicle you arrive in.

Bill Bradley

352. Success is where preparation and opportunity meet.

Bobby Unser

353. Coming together is a beginning; keeping together is progress; working together is success.

Henry Ford

354. Self-belief and hard work will always earn you success.

Virat Kohli

355. Survival was my only hope, success my only revenge.

Patricia Cornwell

356. The secret of your success is determined by your daily agenda.

John C. Maxwell

357. However difficult life may seem, there is always something you can do and succeed at.

Stephen Hawking

358. Your positive action combined with positive thinking results in success.

Shiv Khera

359. Patience, persistence and perspiration make an unbeatable combination for success.

Napoleon Hill

360. Some people dream of success, while other people get up every morning and make it happen.

Wayne Huizenga

361. Put your heart, mind, and soul into even your smallest acts. This is the secret of success.

Swami Sivananda

362. Success is liking yourself, liking what you do, and liking how you do it.

Maya Angelou

363. The first step toward success is taken when you refuse to be a captive of the environment in which you first find yourself.

Mark Caine

364. Develop success from failures. Discouragement and failure are two of the surest steppingstones to success.

Dale Carnegie

365. You are not going to believe this, but you used to fit right here. I'd hold you up and say to your mother: "This kid's going to be the best kid in the world. This kid's going to be somebody better than anybody ever knew." And you grew up good and wonderful. It was great just watching. Every day was like a privilege. Then the time come for you to be your own man and take on the world, and you did. But somewhere along the line, you changed. You stopped being you. You let people stick a finger in your face and tell you you're no good, and when things got hard, you started looking for something to blame. Like a big shadow.

I'll tell you something you already know. The world is not all sunshine and rainbows, it's a very mean and nasty place. And I don't care how tough you are, it will beat you to your knees and keep you there permanently if you let it. You, me or nobody is going to hit as hard as life. But it isn't about how hard you hit. It's about how hard you can get hit and keep moving forward. How much you can take and keep moving forward. That's how winning is done!

Now, if you know what you're worth, get what you're worth, but you got to be willing to take the hits and not pointing fingers, saying you aren't where you want to be because of him or her or anybody! Cowards do that, and that isn't you! You're better than that!

Rocky Balboa